I HAVE A DREAM

AND IT CAN BE YOURS TOO

ANKUR DHIMAN

Made with ♥ on the Notion Press Platform
www.notionpress.com

To Mother Divine, whose boundless grace and strength carried me Here. I Exist to Serve You.

Contents

Preface

This book is more than just my story; it is a manifesto of a purpose I believe has been entrusted to me by Mother Divine. Through every challenge, every revelation, and every word written on these pages, I have felt Her guidance shaping my journey.

I do not claim perfection—in life, in language, or in expression. If there are grammatical missteps, I ask for your understanding. But what I do offer, without hesitation, is truth. Every sentence here comes from the depths of my being, unfiltered and honest.

With humility and gratitude,
Ankur Dhiman

Acknowledgements

With deepest gratitude, I bow to Mother Divine, whose boundless grace and strength guide me. She is the source of my purpose and the force behind every word written here.

I offer my reverence to Lord Bhairava, the guardian of the path, whose presence has given me the courage to walk through darkness and emerge with clarity. His fierce yet compassionate guidance has been a pillar of strength in my transformation.

To my beloved wife, who first endured my way of life and now stands beside me through my struggles—I am eternally grateful.

To my friends, who believed in my vision and stood by me with unwavering support—thank you.

And finally, to you, the reader. By purchasing this book, you have contributed to my cause, and for that, I sincerely thank you.

CHAPTER ONE

At 36, my life looked perfect. The kind of perfect you'd see in a social media post, complete with smiling faces, family vacations, and captions like "Grateful for this life." I had a loving wife, two beautiful kids (They're still there, don't worry), and a steady job that paid the bills. On paper, I was living a life that millions in this country envy. But paper doesn't tell you how heavy perfection feels.

Beneath the surface, my life was a storm—a silent, unrelenting chaos. The cracks were subtle, almost invisible, but they were there—tiny fissures in the very foundation of my existence. No one saw them. Not my family, not my friends, not even me sometimes. But they were there.

I wasn't miserable. I wasn't depressed, exactly. I was just... empty.

It was the kind of emptiness you can't explain to anyone else. Like walking into a room full of people and feeling utterly alone. Like waking up every morning with a vague sense of unease, as if you've forgotten something important but don't know what.

I had everything a man could wish for. And yet, there was nothing.

The only thing that brought me fleeting joy was reading. Fiction novels, specifically. As a child, I devoured comic books, losing myself in the adventures of larger-than-life heroes. As I grew older, my tastes expanded, but the effect remained the same: books were my sanctuary, my escape.

But even that was slipping away.

The grind of daily life—work, family responsibilities, bills to pay—left little room for indulgences like reading. My days were consumed by the monotony of routine: wake up, work, come home, sleep, repeat.

Weekends weren't much better. They weren't restful; they were just a different flavor of busy. Grocery runs, household chores, and endless errands. By Sunday night, I would already be dreading Monday morning.

And yet, I wore the mask. The world saw a man who had it all—an obedient son, a family man, someone who had checked all the right boxes.

But inside, I wanted more. Not just money or success (though I wanted those too). I craved something deeper. Meaning, perhaps. A purpose, maybe. At the time, I didn't know.

And let's not sugarcoat it: I wanted admiration. I wanted to be the guy people pointed to and said, "He's made it." I wanted to be respected, celebrated. But these desires came with their own weight—an ever-present fear of failure, of falling short, of being exposed as a fraud.

Worse still were the darker feelings I rarely admitted to myself. Envy, when a colleague got a promotion. Resentment, when a friend seemed happier in his marriage. Jealousy, when I saw someone post vacation pictures online with captions like, "Living my best life!" I'd scroll through my social media feed, comparing my life to theirs, wondering why their happiness seemed effortless while mine felt like a chore.

It was a silent war inside me. Ambition clashing with insecurity. Hope battling self-doubt. And above all that, the emptiness.

And then, I got a way.

It started innocently, almost imperceptibly. I grew up in a well-to-do family. Money was never a problem. Drinking was a fun indulgence at first, a way to loosen up, to feel lighter. But over the years, it crept into the corners of my life. What had begun as a social habit turned into a private crutch. It had become my go-to after a stressful day at work and eventually, it turned into a nightly ritual. A drink to quiet the thoughts. Another to ease the tension. And another, just because it felt like everything was alright for a moment.

My wife noticed the subtle shifts way before I did. The nights I came to bed later. The mornings I woke up sluggish. The short temper. The distant look in my eyes. She didn't say much, at first. I think she hoped I would realize it myself. That I would see what I was doing.

But I didn't.

Instead, I kept going. I wore the mask, pretending everything was fine while the cracks in my foundation deepened. Alcohol made it easier to ignore the noise in my head, but it also made it harder to act. I felt like everything was fine, yet I was doing absolutely nothing to change the parts of my life that weren't. Just two drinks became four, and four became six.

That's the deceit of alcohol. It makes you vulnerable. It whispers lies that everything is under control while you quietly loosen your grip on reality. By the time I realized what it was doing to me, it was too late. I just couldn't stop.

A night or two without a drink was possible, but those nights would be sleepless. My body would feel restless, my mind racing, and the emptiness I had been numbing would come crashing back with full force. The quiet moments became unbearable as every thought I'd been running from clawed its way to the surface.

The urge to have a drink would only grow stronger the next day, consuming my thoughts until I gave in. It wasn't just a habit anymore —it was a cycle, a relentless loop that tightened its grip on me day by day. And no matter how much I wanted to break free, I felt powerless to do so. Alcohol had become both my escape and my prison.

But I think the mother divine was on my side.

One morning, during my usual hungover, hour-long drive to work, I plugged in Spotify, intending to play some music like I always did. But somehow, a podcast started playing instead. Trust me, I was never a podcast man. I'd never listened to one before, nor did I have any browsing history for such content.

Even now, when my rational mind kicks in and tries to make sense of that day, I can only come up with one explanation. My daughter used to listen to a famous song by Ms. Jaya Kishori on Spotify when we went on drives together. Maybe the algorithm somehow made a connection and directed me to the podcast.

At the time, I didn't overthink it. Hungover and exhausted, I simply let it play. Little did I know, that random moment would plant the seed for something far greater.

The podcast was hosted by Ranveer Allahbadia, and his guest that day was Rajarshi Nandy, who was talking about astrology—planets that rule and govern the way we live. At first, I listened passively, but something he said caught my attention. He spoke about Rahu, the planet often associated with addictions, and how once someone falls under its influence, it's incredibly difficult to break free.

It struck a chord with me. Maybe because, thanks to my wife's interest in astrology, I already knew that Rahu governs the house in my chart that resonates with work and career. Whatever the reason, I found myself drawn in, hanging on every word. I became a fan of that man.

One episode led to another.

In one of the episodes, Rajarshi shared a mantra of Lord Bhairava. He spoke of its power, its ability to bring clarity and transformation to those who chanted it with sincerity. It piqued my curiosity, though at the time, I didn't think much of it beyond fascination.

But one day, all of a sudden, an inspiration came over me, and I started doing the mantra. It wasn't planned, nor did it come with any great resolve. I just felt the urge to begin. One round of 108 chants in the morning and another in the evening became my daily practice. I did it every day, even before my evening ritual—my drinking—began.

At first, it was just something I did, almost mechanical. But somehow, it became a routine, a steady rhythm in my otherwise chaotic life. Over time, my practice deepened. My counts increased from one round to three for both the morning and evening shifts. It felt like I was investing in something greater, though I couldn't yet see what that might be.

Months passed. My life went on as it always had. The same routines, the same struggles, the same emptiness lingering beneath it all.

My wife noticed my chanting but didn't say much about it. She let me be, likely hoping it would bring some change. One evening, however, after I finished chanting and opened my first drink of the night, she teased me. "Maybe you should ask Bhairav to take your habit of drinking away."

I just laughed, brushing it off. Though a small part of me wondered if he could. In the podcast, Rajarshi had said, "You will have to talk to Bhairava with honesty about whatever you want."

The next morning, hungover as usual, as I sat down for my chanting, I closed my eyes, took a deep breath, and spoke to Bhairava — not just as a routine, not just as a mantra, but as though I was speaking to a presence, a guide. With honesty, with vulnerability, I prayed.

"Give me the strength," I whispered, "to let this habit go. Guide me, show me the way."

But nothing miraculous happened. There was no dramatic event, no catastrophic life change, no sudden epiphany. My routine remained the same—if anything, I think it got worse. The drinking continued, and so did the guilt that followed each night. I found myself questioning whether any of it — my chanting, was making a difference at all.

The mornings were still heavy, the nights restless, and the emptiness within me seemed to deepen. Yet, for reasons I couldn't fully understand, I kept going on with my chanting, even as my life felt like it was spiraling further out of control.

And then one day, it all came crashing down.

CHAPTER TWO

My wife, being a government officer, had decided to take a transfer. She knew how the hour-plus-long drive to my workplace was wearing me down, making me more frustrated and irritable with each passing day. She thought that moving closer would ease some of the pressure on me, give me a bit of relief.

Her new station was comparatively near to my workplace. On the surface, it seemed like a solution—less driving, less exhaustion—but deep down, I knew it wasn't the root of my struggles. The drive wasn't the real problem. The cracks in my life ran far deeper than a few extra miles on the road.

Still, I told myself that this change might help, that maybe a shorter commute could give me more time to think, to breathe, to feel something other than the dull ache of routine.

We settled into the new residence we had taken on rent. That night, I went through my usual ritual—drinking until I could numb the day—and then I slept, or at least tried to.

The next morning, my wife left early for her job, leaving me with the task of taking our daughter to her new school for admission. It was supposed to be a simple day, nothing out of the ordinary—just another step in our attempt to create a better routine, a better life.

On my way to my daughter's school, my daughter on the passenger seat and the weight of yet another hungover night pressing down on me, I didn't realize that this seemingly ordinary day would set the stage for something far from routine.

All of a sudden, while laughing at my daughter's joke, my vision blurred for a split second. It was like the world around me flickered, just for an instant, but it was enough. My instincts kicked in, and I slammed on the brakes. The car behind us screeched to a halt, missing ours by mere inches. I could hear the angry honk and the muffled shouts of the driver behind me, but my focus wasn't on them. My hands gripped the steering wheel tightly, my knuckles white. My head was spinning, my chest tightening as though someone had placed a heavy weight on it. My breathing grew rapid and shallow, and my whole body started to shiver uncontrollably and I could hear my heart beating in my ears.

I tried to take in deep breaths, hoping it would calm me down, but it only made things worse. My heart rate quickened, pounding so hard in my chest that I could hear it in my ears. It felt like my chest was caving in, like I couldn't get enough air, and a terrifying thought gripped me: *I'm having a heart attack.*

Panic surged through me, but I knew I had to act. My daughter sat quietly in the passenger seat, wide-eyed, sensing something was wrong. I couldn't let her see me crumble.

Gathering all the courage I could muster, I put the car in gear. My hands trembled as I gripped the wheel, and my body felt weak, but I forced myself to drive. Sprinting towards the nearest hospital, I kept glancing at my daughter to reassure her with a forced smile, even though I could feel fear clawing at my insides.

The journey felt endless, each minute stretching into an eternity as my mind raced with worst-case scenarios. Was this how it was all going to end? My thoughts spiraled, but I clenched the wheel tighter and pressed on. My only focus was getting to the hospital, hoping I wasn't too late.

Finally, I arrived. My hands were still trembling as I parked the car. With my daughter's hand in mine, I ran to the emergency room, my heart still pounding in my chest. The doctor on duty looked up as I burst in, practically blabbering, trying to explain how I was feeling—my chest, my breathing, the dizziness, the shivering. My words tumbled over each other in panic, but he remained calm, listening intently.

"Take a deep breath, son. You are scaring your daughter," he said, gesturing for me to sit down. "Let's figure this out."

He asked me a series of questions, took notes, and examined me carefully with his stethoscope and BP apparatus. His demeanor was steady, almost unnervingly so, but I clung to it like a lifeline.

Next, he called out to a nurse and spoke to her in a low, firm tone. She approached me and asked me to follow her. Still shaky and overwhelmed, I stumbled behind her to the nurse's room, my daughter's hand still clutched tightly in mine.

The nurse gently guided me to a chair. I handed my phone to my daughter so she could stay occupied and asked her to sit beside me. She nodded, her big, concerned eyes fixed on me, but she didn't say a word.

The nurse tied a band around my arm and inserted a cannula into my hand. I winced slightly at the pinch, but the tension in my body was too overwhelming for me to care.

Moments later, a drip was set up, and she administered two successive injections.

The relief was almost immediate. The tightness in my chest began to ease, and the spinning in my head started to settle. My hands stopped trembling, and my breaths came slower, deeper. Doctors are indeed second only to gods.

As I sat there, I could feel my body returning to normal. My heart rate gradually slowed, the panic dissipating with each beat.

It was like emerging from a storm—everything felt calmer, clearer, like I could finally see the horizon after being lost in a sea of chaos.

After a few moments, the doctor returned and looked me squarely in the eyes. “Feeling better now?”

I nodded with a smile on my face and thanks in my eyes.

“You were not having a heart attack,” he said, his tone steady but firm. “It’s called alcohol withdrawal. It’s your body reacting to a lack of alcohol after prolonged use.”

His words hit me like a ton of bricks. Withdrawal? Lack of alcohol?

“But I’m still hungover,” I said, almost bursting into laughter at the absurdity. “I just had drinks last night.”

“Yes,” he said, his tone steady and unwavering. “And you haven’t had a drink since last night. It’s your body demanding it now. This is what alcohol dependency looks like. When the alcohol starts to leave your system, your body reacts violently, needing more.

He paused for a moment, letting his words sink in before continuing, “You’re just one of few who are lucky to experience symptoms very early. Usually, symptoms like these comes too late in the dependency. You must stop or these symptoms will only get worse.”

His words carried a weight that I couldn't ignore. Lucky? That wasn't the word I would've chosen for how I felt in that moment. But as I sat there, absorbing what he had just told me, I realized he was right. This was a warning, an opportunity to take control before things spiraled even further out of reach.

"I'm going to start a treatment protocol that'll help you quit," the doctor added.

"Quit?" I repeated, the word hanging heavy in the air. It wasn't that I hadn't thought about quitting before. I had even tried quitting before. But hearing it framed so bluntly made it feel daunting, monumental. My first instinct was to resist, to tell him I wasn't ready, that I didn't need help. But deep down, I knew the truth—I did need help.

I nodded slowly, not trusting my voice to hold steady. "What does that involve?" I asked hesitantly, the thought of giving up something that had been my crutch for years filling me with equal parts fear and hope.

"I'll put you on medications," he replied. "Monitor your symptoms, manage withdrawal safely. But it's you who will have to quit."

His words made it sound straightforward, almost clinical. But I knew this wasn't going to be easy. The thought of life without alcohol was both liberating and terrifying. Still, I had to start somewhere. This moment, as overwhelming as it felt, might just be the beginning of something new. Something better.

An hour later, I got out from the hospital with a prescription in one of my hands and my daughter's hand in another.

I bought the medicines from the pharmacy and reached out to my car when my cell buzzed.

Wife calling.

"Hello," I picked up the call, my voice still shaky and unsure of how much to tell her about the incident.

"Hello," she said from the other side. "Listen, I called to remind you that today is Krishna Paksha Ashtami. Bring some sweets for your pooja."

I paused for a moment, and then almost burst into laughter — not because of what she said, but at the sheer coincidence of it all. Krishna Paksha Ashtami.

According to Rajarshi Nandy, Krishna Paksha Ashtami is the day of Bhairava — the very deity I had been chanting to every morning and evening, asking for strength, for guidance.

Amusement bubbled up inside me as I tried to process the timing. Of all days, *this* was the one my body choose to revolt. (Though, later my wife told me she had taken a sankalpa to chant certain mantra so i could quit alcoho) But that day, l I looked at the pouch of medicines in my hand and felt like the universe, or perhaps Lord Bhairava himself, was saying,

"Here's the strength. Now quit."

CHAPTER THREE

The next two weeks were worse than hell. Nights were sleepless, haunted by restlessness and racing thoughts that wouldn't let me close my eyes. Days were exhausting, a blur of fatigue and irritability, with my body feeling like it was waging a war against itself.

I lost 10 kilograms of weight in the first week alone, my appetite vanishing as the withdrawal symptoms consumed me. A permanent sense of anxiety settled in, like a constant pressure on my chest that never let up. My heart would race for no reason, my palms perpetually damp with sweat, and every sound or movement around me felt magnified, overwhelming.

The simplest tasks became monumental challenges. My body craved the very thing I was trying to rid myself of, and my mind was in turmoil, questioning whether I could make it through. I felt trapped, like I was sinking deeper into quicksand with every passing day.

And yet, something kept me going. Perhaps it was the mantra I was chanting in the hope of reclaiming myself, or maybe it was the thought of the people I loved who believed I could come out on the other side. Whatever it was, I clung to it desperately, even as my world seemed to crumble around me.

But I persisted with my resolve of never touching alcohol ever in this life or another.

The doctor prolonged my treatment and put me on antidepressants for another two weeks.

A month later, the symptoms somewhat eased. The sleepless nights became less frequent, and the relentless pressure on my chest began to lift. My mind, once clouded with chaos, started to clear, like the fog gradually lifting after a storm. My appetite returned, and food—something I had barely noticed for weeks — suddenly seemed different. Every bite tasted fuller, richer, like I was rediscovering flavors I had long forgotten.

The weight I had lost started to come back, but the change wasn't just physical. My thoughts began transitioning, shifting away from the fearful panic that had gripped me for weeks to something stranger, something unexpected.

I found myself thinking of deities — not in a passing, abstract way, but deeply, almost vividly. It was as if the chaos within me had made space for something else, something ancient and profound. These thoughts weren't forced, nor did they feel intrusive. They simply appeared, often uninvited, yet strangely comforting.

In my free time, I began watching more and more podcasts. I found myself seeking voices that resonated, voices that offered insights and perspectives I had never explored.

Among them, one stood out, just like Rajarshi had. It was the voice of Om Swami — an unconventional monk who lives in the foothills of the Himalayas. There was something magnetic about him. His words carried a simplicity and depth that made spirituality feel approachable, even to someone like me, who was only just beginning to make sense of the chaos within.

His calm demeanor, practical wisdom, and relatable way of explaining the profound drew me in. It wasn't lofty or inaccessible; it felt like he was speaking directly to the questions I didn't even know I had. His teachings weren't about escape—they were about transformation, about facing life head-on with a new perspective.

Intrigued, I quickly devoured all the books written by him. And there I learned about a whole new concept called Sri Vidya.

And I started digging.

It wasn't just another spiritual practice; it was an intricate, powerful tantric tradition rooted in the worship of the divine feminine. It was unlike anything I had encountered before — a blend of devotion, discipline, and profound energy work that seemed to resonate with every fiber of my being.

The only bottleneck was, you must be invited to join this practice.

As I read more, I realized how profound and exclusive this practice was. Sri Vidya wasn't something one could casually stumble into. It required dedication, purity of intent, and a deep commitment to walking a path of inner transformation. And above all you must be invited to join this practice.

It isn't something you could demand or learn from a book alone. You need a guide who could lead you into the intricacies of Sri Vidya, someone who had walked the path themselves and was willing to share their knowledge.

I felt an unexplainable pull toward this path, as though it was calling out to me, even though I didn't know how or when I might be able to access it.

One day, in a burst of hope, I opened Om Swami's website and applied for initiation. I filled out the form with sincerity, pouring my intentions into every word. But I wasn't accepted.

So, I started searching the web relentlessly, going from one website to another, looking for anyone who could guide me.

I found hundreds of websites belonging to various gurus and organizations claiming to teach Sri Vidya. Many of them promised miraculous results, guaranteed enlightenment, or quick access to the secrets of the tradition. But none of them felt right. Not a single one resonated with me.

For some, it was the language they used — it felt overly transactional. For others, it was the prominent placement of payment buttons that immediately discouraged me. The commercialization of something so sacred felt wrong. I wasn't looking to buy a course or learn a skill; I was seeking something far deeper, something authentic and transformative.

So, I decided to take matters in my own hands.

I don't exactly remember the date, but 4 or 5 days before Shukla Paksha Ashtami of the month of May 2024 —a day devoted to the Divine Feminine. On that day, out of nowhere, I felt a spark of inspiration and without overthinking, I took a resolve: I would chant the 32 names of Durga 32 times daily, followed by a homa—a sacred fire ritual from upcoming Shukla Paksha Ashtami till the coming Poornima or full moon.

The decision felt natural, almost as though it wasn't entirely mine but something I was being guided toward. And more so, over the course of my research, I have found that there is no restriction on chanting 32 names of Durga. But there was one problem: I didn't know how to perform a homa. I had sat for Homas many times before, but they were always conducted under the supervision of a priest or someone well-versed in the process. And in this case, I knew in the end after reciting 32 names 32 times, I have to make one oblation with every name but that's just one part, although the main part but one that comes in the middle. I was missing on the beginning and End of a Homa.

Still, the resolve stayed with me, and I knew I couldn't let my ignorance stop me.

I ordered the homa wood online from amazon, along with a small Homa Kunda (A metal Vessel) and in the meanwhile, turned to the web, determined to learn. I scoured YouTube, watching hundreds of videos, searching for anything that could give me a step-by-step manual on how to perform a homa correctly.

But the deeper I searched, the more frustrated I became. The videos were either too superficial or far too advanced, filled with terms and processes that assumed prior knowledge I didn't have. There were rituals explained in bits and pieces, but nothing cohesive—nothing that truly guided someone like me, a novice, someone starting from scratch.

The next day was Shukla Paksha Ashtami. The firewood had arrived, neatly stacked and ready. The Homa Kunda shone brightly in our altar, polished and prepared. Every other small item I thought I would need—ghee, offerings, sacred threads—was in place. Everything was ready.

Except for the most important thing: a manual.

For a moment, I felt utterly defeated. All the effort, all the preparation, and still, I lacked the guidance I so desperately needed. But the inspiration I had felt that day didn't waver. Something inside me whispered that I had to keep going. That this journey of discovery and self-effort was itself part of the practice.

The Divine Feminine, after all, wasn't just about rituals or perfection—it was about devotion, intention, and surrender. And so, I resolved to create my own path, one step at a time.

I picked up a notebook and began to write. I gathered everything I could remember from past experiences and from what I had managed to learn online, piecing it all together into a step-by-step procedure. It was vague, incomplete, and riddled with uncertainties. But at least it was something.

At around 11 PM that night, after carefully arranging all the items in their places, I finally retired to bed. My body was tired, but my mind was restless, brimming with anticipation and questions. Just before shutting my eyes, almost as if on a cue, I picked up my phone and opened YouTube.

The first video on my feed was titled, "Simplest Possible Venkateswara Homa."

Curious, I clicked on it, and as I watched, hope began to flicker inside me. In the description of that video, there was a link to a website: www.vedicastrologer.org.

With a mix of skepticism and excitement, I tapped on the link, and to my utter disbelief, it redirected me to a webpage containing a table—a curated list of Homa manuals for different Hindu deities.

I couldn't believe my eyes. It was exactly what I had been searching for, as if the universe had delivered it to me at the very last moment. I scrolled through the table with trembling fingers, and there it was—a manual for Durga Homa. Not exactly a Homa for 32 Names but it was there. Simplest procedure to the most complex ones. Step by Step.

It felt like divine intervention, as if the Divine Feminine herself had stepped in to guide me, assuring me that I was not alone in this journey. My heart swelled with gratitude as I bookmarked the page, finally feeling prepared for the ritual ahead.

That night, for the first time in days, I drifted off to sleep with a quiet sense of peace.

CHAPTER FOUR

The next day, I woke up before sunrise. The air was cool and still, carrying a sense of calm that seemed to echo the significance of the day ahead. I had a bath, letting the water cleanse not just my body but also my mind, washing away the remnants of doubt and hesitation.

As the first light of dawn began to creep in, I sat down before the Homa Kunda, everything meticulously arranged around me. The firewood was stacked, the ghee bowl was within reach, and the manual from the website was placed neatly beside me for reference.

I took some water in my hand, holding it with reverence, and closed my eyes. In that moment, I felt the weight of my intention—the reason I was doing this. I silently stated my resolve, offering it up with sincerity: "To invoke the blessings of Goddess Durga in the form of my Kul Devi (Family Deity) so she could guide me to the path of Sri Vidya. (Though, I made a special request to the Mother Divine not to make the guidance too dramatic like before.)"

With my intention set, I poured the water onto the floor, signaling the beginning of the ritual.

The days passed as I continued with my resolve. Every morning, I chanted the 32 names of Durga 32 times and followed it with the homa, offering ghee and sacred items into the fire with as much devotion as I could muster. The evenings, I allocated to the chanting of Bhairava mantra.

And yet, once again, nothing extraordinary seemed to happen. The world around me remained the same, and within me, the familiar battle raged on. The occasional episodes of panic attacks would still strike, triggered whenever I missed my medication. They were reminders of the storm I was still navigating, shadows that refused to fade completely.

But despite the lack of immediate miracles, I kept going. Then came Poornima, the day of the full moon, marking the end of my resolve. The ritual concluded without any signs or revelations. No visions, no dramatic shifts, no miraculous guidance.

But as I sat there in the soft glow divine fire, I realized something: completing the ritual itself was the sign. It was something I had seen through to the end, despite the doubts, the struggles, and the lack of immediate results.

By this time, I had seriously started thinking about my career. I had wasted enough time already, caught in a loop of routines and distractions that hadn't taken me anywhere. The thought of where I was headed—or rather where I wasn't—had started to weigh heavily on me.

Working in a privately run educational institution wasn't showing much promise for growth. The opportunities were limited, the future uncertain, and the sense of stagnation had become almost suffocating.

And now, with alcohol out of the picture, I could see things more clearly. The fog that had clouded my judgment for so long was lifting, and for the first time in years, I could truly assess where I stood. The realization wasn't pretty—I had been drifting aimlessly, holding onto a job that felt more like a dead-end than a stepping stone.

My wife, already well-settled in her government service, had been subtly nudging me for a while now. "You should think about starting something of your own," she would say, her tone equal parts supportive and encouraging. "You've got the potential, and you're capable of so much more. Don't worry about the money — I'll support you."

At the times, I had dismissed her words, too caught up in my own haze to take them seriously. But now, they started to make sense. She wasn't just suggesting a change—she was offering me a lifeline, a chance to rebuild and create something meaningful.

The next day after the ritual completed, I was lying in the bed in the evening when my wife asked me to talk to the astrologer whom she was consulting.

"He can guide you about your future," she said. "Ask him if it will be okay to start something of your own."

The man was from Kerala. Though she never met him, she connected with him on Astrotalk App a year or two ago. I knew about him but me being me, I never gave any heed to what he said.

This time, I shrugged, not fully on board, but agreed. "Fine. I'll do it."

She made the chat request and I remained there waiting for his reply but it did not come.

The next day was a holiday or maybe I was on leave I don't fully remember but I was at home when his chat request came. My wife handed over her phone to me.

I shared my birth details and he studied my chart.

"You will be inclined toward spirituality from now on," his text read. "It's there in your chart."

I laughed reading his words. I was sure my wife had discussed my recent mantra-chanting routine with him. Still, for some reason—maybe just to keep the conversation going — I mentioned the ritual I had performed in the name of our Family Deity to seek her blessings.

"Is it Bala?" his text came. "Your Family Deity?"

Frankly, it's just a temple near our home where we used to go. The elders in our family had told us she was our *Kuldevi*, but no one really knew her origins or her name. We simply called it the Jalahu Mata Temple because the place was called Jalahu. (This was also the reason to decide upon 32 names of Durga because in one of the Podcasts I have had heard that no matter the name or original of mother divine all are the incarnations of Durga)

And so, I told him.

"You chart says, It's Bala," His text came.

And then I felt a shiver up my spine.

Bala Tripur Sundari is a Child Goddess who is often regarded as the gateway to Sri Vidya. The very path I was inclined to but wasn't getting any way to enter into.

And on an impulse, I typed, "Can you please guide me upon how to worship her?"

And the reply came in the form of a mantra and instructions. "Chant this mantra 32 times daily."

The moment felt surreal—sacred, even. My eyes welled as I thanked the mother goddess, not just for the mantra but for what it represented: hope. It was as though Bala herself, in her infinite compassion, had reached across the barriers of my doubt and disillusionment to hand me a key. A simple mantra, yes, but also a lifeline. A sign that I was seen, heard, and guided—a thread connecting me to Bala, the gateway I had long sought but never found. I felt a renewed sense of purpose.

Though, I had stumbled upon this moment unexpectedly, it felt anything but accidental. It was as though the Divine had been weaving this connection for years, waiting for me to be ready to take the first step.

The instructions were simple: chant the mantra daily, 32 times. Simple, yet profound. The act of devotion itself became my bridge to something greater. With each repetition, it felt as though I was building a foundation—not only for my connection with the Divine but also for a sense of clarity that had long been missing from my life.

Days turned into weeks, and I embraced the practice with quiet determination. Though, my mantra chanting brought me moments of solace, my external life remained in flux. The weight of stagnation in my career loomed over me, growing heavier with each passing day. I couldn't deny it any longer—my current path wasn't taking me anywhere meaningful. But recognizing the need for change and knowing how to bring about that change were two very different challenges. I found myself at a crossroads, staring into the unknown, unsure of where to turn.

It was during this time that my chanting practice began to evolve. Under the guidance of my wife's astrologer and so-called guru, my simple daily chant transformed into a 25-step ritual practice—a detailed and intricate process, each step performed with precision and intent. What had started as a straightforward act of repetition now demanded much more than mere discipline; it called for unwavering presence, complete surrender, and a depth of focus that, more often than not, I struggled to achieve.

Despite my best efforts, I failed miserably more times than I cared to admit. Each missed step or distracted moment felt like a betrayal of the sacredness of the practice. Yet, even in my failures, there was a lesson—a subtle yet profound reminder that this path wasn't about perfection. It was about persistence, about showing up day after day, no matter how imperfectly. And though I struggled, the practice had an unexpected way of surprising me.

The stillness of those small, fleeting meditative moments during my practice became fertile ground for something deeper to emerge. It was as if the act of devotion, imperfect as it was, had swept away the layers of noise, doubt, and distraction that had long cluttered my mind. In that quiet, something unexpected began to stir—a sense of clarity, a feeling of alignment I hadn't known in years. The ritual, though challenging, seemed to be creating space within me, opening doors I hadn't even realized were closed.

In the silence between chants, where my thoughts softened and my heart quietly opened, something began to take shape — not with fanfare or sudden epiphany, but slowly, like a seed taking root in fertile soil. Each time I sat down to chant, this presence grew stronger — not in words or pictures, but in a feeling, a pull toward something meaningful. There was a quiet certainty in it, as though all the chaos and confusion of my life had been gently rearranging itself to lead me here — to this moment, to this calling that was only just beginning to reveal itself.

CHAPTER FIVE

My journey in education started long before I became a part of the system I would later grow to question.

I had spent my formative years in a govt. run boarding school, where the ideals of discipline, learning, and character-building were deeply ingrained in us. Those years left a profound mark on me, shaping my understanding of what education was meant to be — a transformative force, a gateway to growth and opportunity. Back then, it felt pure, untainted by the cynicism that I would come to encounter years later.

After completing my graduation and post-graduation, I stepped into the world of education not as a student but as an Assistant Professor at a privately run institute. It felt like a natural progression, a way to give back to the field that had shaped me. Standing in front of a classroom, engaging with young minds, and sharing knowledge — it felt meaningful, even fulfilling.

Over the years, my role expanded. I moved from academics to administration, eventually taking on the positions of Director of Admissions and In charge of Finance. These roles gave me a front-row seat to the inner workings of the institution — an unfiltered view of its policies, priorities, and, most unsettlingly, its flaws. I began to see a side of education that I had been shielded from as a student and even as a professor.

At first, I told myself that what I was seeing was just a natural part of running any large organization — inevitable compromises, the kind of trade-offs required to keep things running smoothly. But as time went on, I realized these weren't isolated incidents or unfortunate necessities; they were part of a systemic problem. The deeper I got into administration, the more I saw the cracks in the foundation of what we were calling "education."

I started witnessing firsthand the darker sides of the system. Teachers and staff were underpaid, expected to deliver extraordinary results with minimal resources, while the institution itself prioritized profit margins above all else. Students were treated not as learners but as revenue streams, their worth measured in fees rather than potential. Education was no longer about nurturing minds or fostering growth — it was a business. A product to be marketed, sold, and packaged in glossy brochures with grand promises.

As Director of Admissions, I was part of the machinery that brought students into this system. I sat in meetings where decisions about quotas and marketing strategies were discussed with the detached language of financial targets. I managed the budgets, seeing firsthand how resources were allocated — not to improve the quality of education but to maximize profit margins. I was part of a system where education had been reduced to a commodity, stripped of its transformative purpose.

This wasn't just a problem confined to the institution I worked for. As I began to research, I discovered it was everywhere. Across the country, countless so-called educational institutions were run not by educators or visionaries but by businessmen looking for a legal way to circulate their money. These institutions weren't built on the ideals of learning or growth; they were built on the principles of profit and exploitation. Teachers were disposable, students were customers, and education was just another transaction.

The more I uncovered, the more disillusioned I became. The ideals I had grown up with, the principles I had carried into my career, felt like distant memories. Education, in its truest sense, is about transformation — it's about opening minds, fostering curiosity, and equipping individuals with the tools to navigate life with purpose and confidence. But here, it had become hollow, a shiny facade masking an empty core.

And then, the guilt began to creep in — slowly at first, like a whisper in the back of my mind, and then louder, until it was impossible to ignore. I realized that I was a part of this system. For years, I had worked within it, playing my role, signing papers, and making decisions that perpetuated the very flaws I had come to despise. I wasn't complicit in intention, but I was complicit in action. Every day that I showed up, I fed the machine, and the realization gnawed at me.

I began to see my actions, or lack thereof, through a harsher lens. How many students had I watched being treated as customers instead of learners? How many brilliant teachers had I seen leave because they couldn't survive on the meager salaries offered? How many times had I shrugged off these issues as "just the way things are"? The answers left me restless, and for the first time, I couldn't ignore the weight of my own inaction.

It wasn't that I hadn't cared — I had always wanted to do better, to be better. But I was helpless. I was just an employee. I had convinced myself that one person couldn't make a difference, that my role was too small to matter.

Now, as mind cleared, I saw those justifications for what they were: excuses. And they no longer held up.

I think that's what divine blessings do to one's mind—they untangle the web of confusion we often create for ourselves. Slowly, quietly, they shine a light on the shadows we've grown comfortable in, forcing us to confront the truths we've ignored. The very mind that had once convinced me that everything was justified now rebelled against its own reasoning. It began to demand change, to push me toward a new way of seeing, a new way of being.

The guilt wasn't just about my role in the system; it was about my silence, my passivity. Every time I turned a blind eye, I let down the students or parents who had trusted us with their kid's futures and the teachers who gave their all despite being undervalued. That realization was heavy, but it wasn't paralyzing — it was galvanizing. It pushed me to think, to dream, and to imagine what could be different.

The more I engaged in my ritual, the more I couldn't stop thinking about it. Every day, the idea grew louder in my mind. What if I could create something different? An institution where education was truly about learning, growth, and empowerment? A place where teachers were respected and fairly compensated, and where students were nurtured as individuals rather than treated as sources of revenue?

It felt ambitious, almost audacious, but it was a spark—a vision that refused to be ignored. Bala's mantra gave me a sense of inner connection, and this idea of creating an institution began to feel like the external manifestation of that connection. Perhaps this was the path the Divine had been preparing me for all along.

So, I started researching.

Building an educational institution in India is no small feat. It's not as simple as renting a building, hiring teachers, and admitting students. The process is heavily regulated, layered with bureaucracy, and, in many ways, riddled with contradictions.

To begin with, any such institution must legally operate as a not-for-profit entity i.e. as a society or a Trust. On paper, this sounds noble — a safeguard to ensure that education remains a sacred service and not a business. But in reality, the system has been distorted beyond recognition.

The concept of a not-for-profit educational institution in India is an ironic one. While these entities are legally required to reinvest all their earnings into the institution itself, the promoters often find ways to generate substantial profits behind the scenes. The loopholes are glaring. For instance, many promoters of such institutions set up separate business entities under the name of family members or close associates to provide services to the school or college — whether it's leasing land, running canteens, or managing transportation. These services are billed at exorbitant rates, effectively siphoning off money while maintaining the appearance of a not-for-profit entity. It's a legal shell game, one that allows promoters to amass wealth while ostensibly complying with regulations.

As I delved deeper into this, the absurdity of the situation became clear. Here I was, imagining an institution built on genuine principles of learning and empowerment, while the system seemed almost designed to reward those who gamed it. The very structure that was supposed to uphold the sanctity of education had become a means for wealth circulation and profit-making — only this time, disguised in the language of charity.

Beyond the legal and ethical complexities, there was the sheer financial magnitude of the task. Education, particularly in its initial stages, is capital-intensive. Even with the most minimal resources — a modest building, basic infrastructure, and a small but competent staff — the investment required would run into crores. Land acquisition alone, especially in urban or semi-urban areas, could cost a fortune. Add to that the costs of construction, equipment, faculty salaries, and operational expenses, and the figures quickly became overwhelming.

The reality was sobering. To create an institution that truly prioritized education over profit required not just vision but substantial financial backing. I wasn't a business tycoon or someone with a surplus of wealth to invest. The numbers on paper seemed insurmountable. And yet, the vision refused to leave me. Despite the absurdity, despite the odds, I couldn't shake the feeling that this was the path I was meant to walk.

I realized that this journey would demand more than just passion — it would require strategy, resilience, and an unshakable commitment to the ideals I wanted to uphold. The system was daunting, yes, but the clarity I had gained through my spiritual practice gave me the strength to believe that somehow, some way, it could be done.

CHAPTER SIX

By this time, i was already over the withdrawl phase. The Doctor had declared me medicines free. And the newfound purpose left me both energized and overwhelmed. For the first time in years, I felt like I had direction, like I was finally moving toward something that mattered. But the enormity of the task before me—building an institution that would embody the true spirit of education—felt staggering. Purpose is a powerful thing, but without a plan, it can become paralyzing. And so, I found myself asking the simplest yet most difficult question: *Where do I begin?*

So, I turned to the one person who had stood by me through every storm — my wife. I explained my vision to her, baring my soul in a way I hadn't done before. I told her about my dream of creating an institution rooted in values, one that honored the divine inspiration I had received during my journey of transformation. I wanted to build something lasting, something that would touch lives and give back to society.

At first, she listened quietly. I could see the wheels turning in her mind as she weighed the enormity of what I was proposing. When I finished, there was a long silence, and for a moment, I wondered if I had overwhelmed her.

But as always, she nodded in a yes.

The next step in my journey was a practical one: registering a not-for-profit organization. After careful deliberation and weighing all the options, I chose to establish a Trust instead of a Society. The decision wasn't made lightly. A Trust, unlike a Society, grants its Trustees greater authority over its affairs, and this autonomy resonated deeply with the vision I had for what I wanted to create.

With all my heart and unwavering dedication, I poured myself into crafting the Trust Deed—a document that would become the foundation of how the Trust would operate. Every clause, every word, was meticulously thought out, ensuring that the guiding principles of fairness and accountability were enshrined at its very core.

One of the most significant inclusions was the Remuneration Policy. I was determined that the Trust would operate ethically, ensuring that no individual employed by it would ever be paid below the minimum wages specified by the Government at any given time. This wasn't just about compliance; it was about dignity—recognizing the value of every individual's contribution and ensuring that no one was exploited under the guise of noble intentions.

I also introduced clear structures for salaries, including the remuneration of the Chairman of the Board of Trustees. There were ceilings put in place for withdrawals to ensure that the Trust's funds would always be utilized responsibly and in alignment with its mission. This wasn't just a document of rules—it was a testament to the values and purpose that had driven me to take this step in the first place. It reflected the belief that an organization built for a higher cause must embody the integrity and fairness it seeks to promote in the world.

As I finalized the Trust Deed, I couldn't help but feel a deep sense of fulfillment. It was more than a legal requirement—it was the first tangible manifestation of my dream, a step toward creating something that would outlive me and continue to serve its purpose for generations to come.

Next, I pooled together all my available resources and came up with ₹11,000. It wasn't much, but it was enough to open the first bank account for the trust. I named it **Sri Bala Gurukulam Foundation Trust**, in honor of the Divine Mother, whose guidance had brought me to this point.

Walking into the bank with my meager amount felt humbling, almost surreal. As I signed the papers and watched the cashier count the notes, I felt a strange mix of emotions — hope, fear, and a quiet determination. ₹ 11,000 wasn't just money; it was a symbol of a new beginning, a seed planted in the fertile ground of faith.

While the Trust was being set up, I spent my free time thinking, scribbling notes, and staring into space as I tried to make sense of the mountain ahead of me. I knew the dream wasn't just about creating an institution; it was about creating a space where students could grow, where teachers could thrive, and where the soul of education could be restored. But as noble as that vision was, it also came with a harsh reality: I needed money. Building anything in this world — especially something meaningful — required resources.

And I had none.

The clarity I had gained from my spiritual journey helped me see this challenge for what it was: a necessary step. If I wanted to manifest this dream, I needed to focus on the practicalities before the idealism. So, I shifted my focus toward a single question: *How can I generate the funds to take the first step?*

The answer didn't come immediately. I toyed with different ideas, ranging from loans to partnerships, but each one felt wrong. I didn't want the vision to be compromised by outside influences or financial pressures. More so, I did not have anything to hypothecate to the banks and the Government schemes, all catered to for-profit institutions.

One evening, as I reflected on my strengths, the idea came to me. Education was my domain. I had spent years immersed in it, as a student, a professor, and an administrator. I understood its intricacies, its challenges, and its potential. And then it struck me: I could create a video lecture series for the Navodaya Vidyalaya Screening Test.

The idea made sense. As an alumnus of a Navodya Vidyalya, I understood the unique challenges faced by students preparing for such exams. My experience gave me an edge — an insider's understanding of what it took to succeed. If I could package that knowledge into an accessible, high-quality lecture series, it could not only help students but also generate the funds needed to fuel my larger vision.

When I shared the idea with my wife, she gave me a look that was equal parts skepticism and cautious support.

"Do you really think this will work?" she asked. "There's a lot of competition out there, and the market is niche."

Her concerns were valid, but there was something in her tone that told me she believed in me, even if she wasn't sure about the idea. A few days later, she handed me an iPad.

"You'll need this to make the videos," she said simply. That gesture floored me. It wasn't just a gift — it was her way of saying, *I trust you. I believe in you.*

With the iPad in hand, I threw myself into the work. The idea was pretty simple. Sell Videos for a price an average middle-class parents could afford and the proceeds will go to fuel my dream.

So, I outlined the syllabus, created lesson plans, and began recording trial videos. The process was far from easy. I wasn't a natural in front of the camera, and the first few recordings felt awkward and stilted. But I kept at it, refining my approach, learning from my mistakes, and slowly finding my voice.

My free time, once spent scrolling through social media or lost in distractions, was now dedicated to this project. Evenings became a blur of editing, scripting, and recording. There were moments of frustration when the technology wouldn't cooperate, or when my self-doubt crept in, whispering that this was all a waste of time. But every time I pressed record; I felt a flicker of hope — a reminder of why I had started this journey in the first place.

My wife watched me with a mix of quiet pride and lingering skepticism. "I hope this works out," she said one night as I edited a particularly challenging video. "Not just for us, but for you."

Her words stayed with me. This wasn't just about funding the dream; it was about proving to myself that I could take an idea and turn it into something real.

The lecture series wasn't perfect — it was a work in progress, like me. But it was a beginning. It was the first step toward something larger than myself, something that had the potential to change lives. And though the road ahead was uncertain, one thing was clear: the journey had finally begun.

But creating the lectures was only one part of the puzzle. The bigger challenge loomed ahead: *How do I get these lectures to the parents who want their kids to prepare for the exam?* It was one thing to create the content; it was another to deliver it to the right audience.

I began researching ways to distribute the lectures. After days of scouring the internet, I came across an online Learning Management System (LMS) that offered a one-stop solution. It provided me with both a website and a mobile app—a digital storefront where parents could access the lectures. The platform promised ease of use, professional presentation, and seamless payment options. It felt like the perfect solution.

Excited, I jumped onto it without hesitation. I spent weeks uploading my videos, designing the website, and tailoring the app to make it user-friendly. It was thrilling to see my hard work come to life in such a tangible way. When the series was finally launched, I felt a surge of pride. The iPad had been put to good use, and my vision was no longer just an idea—it was real, accessible, and ready to make an impact.

But then came the next question: *How do I convince parents to subscribe for my lecture series?*

I was an educator, not a sales expert. Marketing, branding, and customer outreach, though concepts I had taught in classrooms, were very different when it came to putting them into practice. Back when I had served as Director of Admissions, I had a hefty budget, a dedicated team, and the institutional backing to drive results. Here, I had none of that.

It was just me, a handful of videos, and a platform waiting for an audience.

CHAPTER SEVEN

After days of brainstorming and exploring different strategies, I decided to harness the vast reach and influence of social media. With its unparalleled ability to connect with specific audiences and engage with them directly, social media seemed like the perfect solution to spread the word and attract attention to my cause. It was a modern, dynamic tool that promised to amplify my efforts and reach parents and stakeholders in ways traditional methods couldn't.

I created a Facebook page and a YouTube channel, sending out invites to my social circle to build some initial momentum. The first demo video I posted seemed like a breakthrough — it gained a lot of traction, drawing congratulations and best wishes from friends and well-wishers. Calls started pouring in, and for a brief moment, it felt like the beginning of something big.

And then, just as quickly as it has begun, everything died down. The buzz faded, the calls stopped, and the engagement dwindled. What had seemed like a promising start now felt like a false dawn, leaving me grappling with the reality that I needed to rethink my approach yet again.

So, I tried running ads on social media, targeting parents in relevant regions, but they barely made a dent. The clicks were few, and conversions were almost zero. I was exhausting my resources. I reached out to friends and family, asking them to spread the word, but the results were underwhelming. In desperation, I even attempted cold calls to parents and school groups, but those efforts only led to awkward conversations and polite rejections.

Nothing worked. The hard truth hit me like a brick wall

The coaching business was an entirely different world, one I had never truly understood. It wasn't just about the quality of the content—it was about perception, branding, and the ability to convince parents that their child's future depended on your product. It was a ruthless marketplace driven by aggressive marketing, flashy promises, and larger-than-life reputations. My idealistic belief in the power of good education clashed harshly with this reality.

Each failed attempt left me more disheartened than the last. My evenings, once filled with purpose and creativity, were now consumed by frustration and self-doubt. I questioned everything — my abilities, my decisions, and even the dream itself. Was I cut out for this? Had I overestimated myself? The weight of failure threatened to crush the determination that had carried me this far.

But in those dark moments, I also began to understand something important. This wasn't just a failure; it was a lesson. I realized that while my purpose and passion were strong, they weren't enough on their own. If I wanted to succeed, I needed to step out of my comfort zone and learn the skills I lacked.

So, I started learning.

Social media advertising stood out as a beacon of hope, promising voracious results on a tight budget. It was a skill I didn't have but desperately needed. With no team, no budget, and no time to waste, I rolled up my sleeves and dove into the world of digital marketing.

My Facebook feed seemed to transform overnight. It became a carnival of promises, with countless educators and "marketing experts" claiming they could make me a social media advertising guru for just ₹99. "Unlock the secrets to earning ₹1 crore in your coaching business in just one month!" the ads screamed, accompanied by flashy thumbnails and testimonials of supposed students holding oversized cheques.

And in my desperation, I fell for it.

I signed up for one course after another, believing that maybe — just maybe — this would be the one that taught me the magic formula. But what I found was the same recycled advice, dressed up in different packaging. These so-called "experts" rarely offered more than superficial tips, and the promises of instant success were nothing more than pipe dreams. The cycle became frustratingly predictable: I'd purchase the course, skim through the materials, and come away with nothing useful except a lighter wallet.

But it didn't stop there.

Because one thing I was convinced of was that social media advertising actually works. I had seen it with my own eyes. I was a firsthand witness to its power — thanks to the courses I bought. The problem wasn't with the concept; it was with me. I didn't know how to harness it effectively. That realization further fueled my desperation to crack the code.

Soon, my YouTube feed followed the same pattern I'd seen on Facebook, flooding me with videos from self-proclaimed experts giving business advice. They flaunted screenshots of their Amazon platforms or PayPal accounts, showcasing earnings in thousands of dollars, and claimed it was all thanks to their "foolproof" methods. It was a spectacle — part performance, part manipulation—designed to lure in people like me: desperate to make an impact, eager for a breakthrough, and willing to believe in the next big promise.

And I fell for it.

Again and again, I tried one thing after another, chasing their suggestions, hoping to replicate their success. I signed up for additional courses, downloaded free resources, and took copious notes from "business gurus" who seemed to have cracked the code. I watched hours of tutorials, scribbled out strategies in my notebook, and poured over case studies with the intensity of a man searching for a lifeline. Each time, I thought, *this is it. This is the one that will change everything.*

My wife's faith in me was visibly fading by now. The trust she had once placed in my ability to make this work was eroding, replaced by a quiet skepticism that hurt more than her words ever could.

One evening, after yet another unsuccessful attempt at launching an ad campaign, she confronted me. Her voice was calm but firm, carrying the weight of her growing frustration.

"You're dreaming to become a king but you neither have a kingdom nor the resources to build one," she said.

The words stung, cutting through the layers of hope and determination I had wrapped myself in. As much as I wanted to dismiss them, I couldn't deny the truth in what she was saying. From her perspective, I was chasing grand dreams with nothing tangible to show for my efforts—just a growing list of failures and dwindling resources.

"You need to start small," she continued, her tone softening, as though she was trying to cushion the blow. "You're putting everything into these big ideas that aren't working. Build something manageable first, and then grow it."

I wanted to argue, to tell her that starting small wasn't an option, that my vision demanded more. But deep down, I knew she was only trying to help, to guide me back to a more realistic path. Still, I couldn't shake the feeling that starting small would mean surrendering the dream.

But each time, I came out of it with the same result: a lighter wallet and an increasingly heavier sense of frustration.

In my desperation, I turned to what felt like actionable steps. I rebranded my application couple of times, convinced that a fresh look and a new logo would attract parents. I tweaked my website endlessly, adding features, refining the interface, and redesigning layouts to make it look more professional. I even invested in Canva Pro, thinking better graphics and more polished designs for my ads would finally grab the attention I needed.

Each tweak felt like a step forward. It gave me a fleeting sense of control, a momentary hope that this time things would be different. But in the end, none of it worked. No amount of rebranding or redesigning could solve the deeper issue: I wasn't reaching the right audience in the right way. I was trapped in a cycle of superficial fixes, masking the fact that I lacked the foundational skills to truly connect with the market I was trying to serve.

Every failure felt heavier than the last. The frustration built up like a tidal wave, threatening to pull me under. My confidence began to erode, piece by piece, as I wondered if I was just fooling myself — if the dream I was chasing was even attainable.

Despite all my failures, every morning, when I sat for my practice, the vision of my dream became more vivid, almost as if it were teasing me to hold on. I could see the institute clearly in my mind—the architectural design, the vibrant campus alive with energy, and the carefully crafted system it would follow to nurture young minds. It felt real, tangible, and within reach.

However, whenever I opened my eyes, reality hit me like a cruel reminder. All I had was a website—bare, lifeless, where the sole visitor was me.

One day, while scrolling the YouTube, I came across a video explaining what AI could do, and just like that, another idea took shape in my mind. Desperation is a cruel teacher, but it also forces you to think outside the box. The competitive exam preparation market was massive, and the number of candidates even larger. Navodya Vidyalya Entrance Prep was a Niche, the end user was in class fifth. The scopes were limited. But in the adult market, the scope felt endless.

With new insights into AI's capabilities, I decided to take a different approach: I would use AI to create study materials.

And, so I began by generating comprehensive notes for the CTET (Central Teacher Eligibility Test) examination using ChatGPT. Because it was the exam that a month away. And every year lakhs of candidates sit for this exam.

Creating notes was a meticulous process, tweaking and refining the content to ensure it was accurate, relevant, and user-friendly. Once I was satisfied, I uploaded the notes to my website. This felt like a fresh start — a way to offer something more expansive and valuable to potential learners.

Whatever I had learned about social media advertising finally began to pay off. I used targeted campaigns to promote the notes and courses, and soon the leads started to trickle in. It wasn't a flood, but it was progress. For every lead I captured, I nurtured it personally, following up with calls, answering questions, and building trust.

But the process wasn't easy. On average, only 1 out of 30 leads converted into a sale. The cost of conversion was painfully high, both in terms of money and effort. Every sale felt like a small victory, but the math just didn't add up. And soon, I hit the bottleneck.

No matter how hard I tried to optimize, my costs were far higher than my sales. The ads, the time spent nurturing leads, the constant back-and-forth — all of it drained my resources faster than the sales could replenish them. It was like pouring water into a leaking bucket.

The harsh reality set in: this model wasn't sustainable. I was putting in everything I had, but instead of moving forward, I felt like I was running in places — spending more than I was earning, and inching closer to a breaking point.

But then I asked: *How are others sustaining?*

There were literally hundreds of ed-tech companies out there, thriving — or so it seemed. If I was struggling so much to make ends meet, how were they managing to operate on such a grand scale? The curiosity gnawed at me, and once again, my research began.

And once again, I hit a harsh truth: the ed-tech industry wasn't as glamorous as it appeared on the surface. Behind the polished apps, high-quality advertisements, and aggressive marketing strategies was a web of complex business dynamics. Many of these companies weren't running on profits — they were running on raised capital and debt, fueled by the hope of someday turning a profit. They attracted investors with big promises, secured funding, and poured money into marketing and expansion, even if it meant bleeding cash in the process. It was a long game of high risk, and only a handful would ever emerge successful.

The deeper I dug, the clearer the picture became. This wasn't just a business; it was a cutthroat market where survival often depended on who could burn the most money while waiting for results. Companies were fighting tooth and nail for market share, slashing prices, offering massive discounts, and flooding social media with ads to outpace their competition. Again, it wasn't just about the quality of education anymore — it was about who could shout the loudest and stay in the game the longest.

And here I was. Alone. My modest operation, built on the pure intent of raising money for my dream, was competing against giants armed with armies of marketers, investors, and resources, driven by one thing — profit.

The gap felt insurmountable.

And it forced me to confront a painful question: *Am I even heading in the right direction?*

My aim had never been to create just another profit-making machine. The vision that had driven me from the start — the vision I saw so vividly in my moments of clarity — was to build an institution. A place that stood as a sanctuary for young minds, driven by values and a genuine desire to make a difference. This wasn't the purpose that had inspired me during my quiet moments of reflection.

My dream wasn't about accumulating wealth or chasing trends. It was about creating something meaningful, something that would outlast me and leave a real impact on the world. But here I was, caught in a system that seemed to demand everything but meaning. The stark contrast between my purpose and my methods gnawed at me, leaving me conflicted.

I felt like a visionary who dreams of ending corruption after winning the election but is trying to raise the money to fight that election by indulging in the very corruption he wishes to destroy. The irony was suffocating, and the disconnect between my intentions and my actions felt like a betrayal of my own ideals.

How could I hope to create something pure and transformative when the path I was treading was riddled with compromises and shortcuts? How could I hold onto my vision if I let the means to achieve it undermine its very foundation? These questions loomed over me, heavy and unrelenting, forcing me to confront the uncomfortable truth: I was losing sight of what truly mattered.

And in that moment, I realized that if I wanted to honor the vision that had ignited this journey, I needed to change course — not just in action, but in mindset. I couldn't let the system dictate my path. I needed to find a way to stay true to my values, even if it meant starting over.

CHAPTER EIGHT

Shutting down everything, I decided to start afresh.

But where should I start from?

Once again, I resorted to the web, searching for the origins of famous institutions. How did they start? Who were the visionaries behind them? What challenges did they face?

As I delved deeper, one story stood out — a story that resonated deeply with my own inner conflict and aspirations. It was the story of Banaras Hindu University (BHU) and its founder, Pandit Madan Mohan Malaviya.

BHU, now one of the most prestigious universities in India, wasn't built on government grants or corporate funding. It was the dream of a single man who believed in the transformative power of education. Malaviya envisioned An Institution that blended India's ancient wisdom with modern knowledge, creating individuals who were not only intellectually capable but also spiritually grounded.

At the time, education in India was either rooted in traditional gurukuls, which lacked modern relevance, or restricted to colonial institutions that alienated students from their cultural heritage. Malaviya dreamed of bridging this gap. But the dream was audacious, almost impossible. He had no institutional backing, no massive funding, and no precedent to follow.

What he did have, however, was unwavering faith and a determination to rally people to his cause. He began by traveling across the country, appealing to the public for support. His speeches were impassioned, touching on the need for self-reliance and the revival of Indian culture through education. Malaviya didn't limit his efforts to elite circles; he approached everyone — merchants, farmers, industrialists, and even common laborers—asking for donations, no matter how small.

The people responded. Some gave money; others donated land or materials. Even more inspiring, many offered their time and labor. It wasn't just Malaviya's vision that built BHU—it was the collective belief of a nation that education could be the foundation of freedom and progress.

But the journey wasn't easy. Malaviya faced skepticism, political challenges, and logistical hurdles. Yet, he persisted. There was even a famous incident. One day, Pandit Malviya visited a wealthy businessman's shop and humbly requested a contribution for the university. Instead of responding kindly, the shopkeeper insulted him and, in a fit of arrogance, spat in Malaviya's outstretched hands.

Without showing any anger or resentment, Malaviya calmly wiped his hands and said, "This was for me. Now, what will you give for the university?"

The shopkeeper was stunned by Malaviya's patience and humility. Overcome with shame and admiration for his noble cause, he immediately donated a generous amount for BHU.

Malaviya's story made me pause. It wasn't just the grandeur of BHU that inspired me — it was the humility of its beginnings. It reminded me that even the grandest visions start with a single step, a single voice daring to ask for change.

I found similar inspiration in the story of Rabindranath Tagore's Visva-Bharati University in Santiniketan. Tagore, too, envisioned an institution that transcended the limitations of colonial education. He sought to create a space where students could learn in harmony with nature, exploring not just academic subjects but also art, culture, and spirituality. Tagore funded the institution largely through his own resources and public support, demonstrating a deep personal commitment to his vision.

Another remarkable example was the Aligarh Muslim University, founded by Sir Syed Ahmad Khan. Like Malaviya, Sir Syed believed that education was the key to empowering a community. He faced immense opposition from conservative factions within his own community, yet he persevered. He wrote tirelessly, campaigned across the country, and appealed to both Indian and British audiences to support his cause.

These stories shared a common thread: the founders didn't wait for external approval or ideal conditions. They relied on the power of conviction and community. They weren't afraid to ask for help, to involve the public in their mission, and to persist even when success seemed uncertain.

As I read about these visionaries, something clicked within me. Their stories weren't just history lessons; they were blueprints. They taught me that starting afresh didn't mean starting alone. It meant building something that resonated with others, something that people could believe in and contribute to.

I began to reflect on my own vision. Could I, too, create something that would inspire people to rally together? Could I turn my frustrations with the education system into a force for change? The thought was daunting, but these pioneers had faced far greater challenges. Their stories gave me courage—the courage to take the first step, however small, and trust that the rest would follow.

The spark had been lit. Now, it was time to fan the flames.

But before I go any further, I think now is the best time to tell you about my family, where I come from, and the values that shaped me.

CHAPTER NINE

I was born and brought up in a middle-class family in Himachal Pradesh. My father, now retired, was a Medical Officer with the Government of Himachal Pradesh. His career is defined not just by his skill as a doctor but also by his unwavering commitment to honesty and compassion. But the story that continues to inspire me the most is that of my grandfather, Ishwar Dass Dhiman, my father's father.

He began his career as a humble schoolteacher back in sixties, eventually rising to the position of Headmaster. Teaching wasn't just a job for him — it was a calling. He believed that education was the most powerful tool to transform lives, and he lived by that principle every single day.

It was entirely by accident that he found himself drawn into politics. After retiring as a Headmaster, he was approached by members of the community who admired his integrity and leadership. They urged him to run for office, believing that his moral compass and dedication to public service were exactly what the state needed. Reluctantly at first, and then with growing conviction, he stepped into the political arena.

But even as he became a two-time Education Minister in the Government of Himachal Pradesh, my grandfather remained steadfastly true to his principles. He wasn't a politician in the traditional sense. He didn't play games or make empty promises. He wasn't concerned with power or wealth. He saw politics as an extension of his service to the community—a platform to uplift the people and improve the education system he so deeply cared about.

His life was a testament to simplicity and humility. When he retired from his teaching career and decided to fight his first election, he lived in a small 10-by-10 room made of clay bricks. It was modest, unadorned, and entirely reflective of the man he was. Over the course of his long political career, his name became synonymous with honesty and uprightness. People respected him not just for his position but for the values he embodied.

But it would be a lie to tell you that I have only ever admired him for his honesty. The pull of the desires of the material world is so strong that it can consume one's soul completely. There were times when I loathed him for his integrity. Growing up, I often felt the weight of his principles in ways that made me uncomfortable, even resentful.

When my friends teased me about the frugal lifestyle I lived, I sometimes wished my grandfather had been more like the other politicians they imagined—men who wielded their power and wealth with ease. Or when they challenged me with taunting words, suggesting that if their grandfather had been a minister, they would have access to all the luxuries they associated with that status.

Even during my graduation, there were times when people refused to believe that I was the grandson of a minister.

"You're lying," they would say, pointing out my simple clothes and the modest way I carried myself. Not that I did not want the luxuries but because of the resources I had on my disposal. (Sometimes, I now think it could have been the reason of my indulgence in alcohol. But that chapter is over now.) Whatever the reason, my lifestyle simply didn't align with the image of how politicians or their families are often perceived in this country.

And I would be lying if I said it didn't hurt. There were moments when I envied the effortless privilege that other kids seemed to enjoy, kids whose parents weren't ministers but wielded more wealth than I could dream of. There were times when I questioned why my family couldn't have taken advantage of the power my grandfather once held. Why couldn't we have lived in a sprawling house, driven flashy cars, or enjoyed the privileges that seemed to come so easily to others?

But now the same values I once questioned are now the ones I hold closest to my heart. The funeral ground where my grandfather's last rites were performed was the testament that true wealth isn't measured in material possessions or the size of your bank account — it's measured in the impact you have on others, the integrity with which you live, and the legacy you leave behind.

Yes, his honesty came at a cost. It meant that we lived simply, often frugally. It meant that we weren't part of the social circles that flaunted their connections and wealth. But it also meant that we carried forward a name that stood for something far greater than riches or power.

Now, as I reflect on my own journey, I see his influence everywhere. His life serves as both a guide and a challenge — pushing me to dream big but stay grounded, to build something meaningful without compromising my values. And even during times when the temptations of the world pull at me, I remind myself of his unwavering commitment to living a life of purpose.

Now, coming back to the question of gathering public support, I knew I wasn't Madan Mohan Malaviya or Rabindranath Tagore. I wasn't a renowned figure with the power to inspire the masses through speeches or sheer charisma. But I did have something else — a legacy. My grandfather's life of service had touched countless lives during his time in politics, and I thought, perhaps, I could reach out to the people he had helped.

It seemed like a logical place to start. My grandfather, during his stint in politics, had gone out of his way to support the community. Whether it was improving schools, helping individuals secure jobs, or simply offering a listening ear to those in need, he had been a man of the people. Surely, I thought, these same people would still hold his memory in high regard and might be willing to support a cause.

But reality has a strange way of shattering our illusions.

When I started reaching out, I quickly realized how much things had changed. The people my grandfather had helped decades ago were no longer the struggling families and young hopefuls he had once supported. Many of them were now successful businessmen, well-established and wielding significant influence. They were no longer the wide-eyed individuals who had once looked up to him for guidance. Instead, they were pragmatic, calculating, and deeply entrenched in the world of profits and returns.

Conversations that I thought would be heartwarming tributes to my grandfather's legacy turned out to be cold, transactional exchanges. "That's a noble idea," one of them said after I explained the vision for my trust. "But what's in it for me?"

I was taken aback. In their eyes, everything had become an equation — investments, returns, benefits. They weighed my words not in terms of values or principles but in terms of profit and loss. The altruism my grandfather had once embodied seemed like a distant memory, a relic of a time they had long outgrown.

And then there were the ones who welcomed me with open arms, smiling faces, warm assurances, and promises of unwavering support. They listened attentively, nodded in agreement, and showered me with words of encouragement. “What a beautiful idea,” they would say, or, “Your grandfather would be proud of you.” Their words lit brief flickers of hope within me.

But as days turned into weeks, their promises proved hollow. Calls went unanswered, messages ignored, and meetings postponed indefinitely. Some came up with excuses — pressing business commitments, financial constraints, or simply a lack of time. Others didn’t bother with explanations at all.

Each encounter left me more disillusioned than the last. These were the same people who had once stood on the shoulders of my grandfather’s generosity, who had built their success on the foundation of his selfless service. Yet, here they were, unwilling — or perhaps unable — to look beyond their immediate interests.

The rejections hurt, but the false assurances hurt even more. At least the straightforward “No” of the businessmen felt honest, if cold. But the empty promises? They were like a knife wrapped in silk, cutting deeper with every instance of misplaced hope.

It broke me. I felt as though I was wading through quicksand, sinking deeper with every step I tried to take. The weight of disappointment began to crush me, and doubt crept into my mind like an unwelcome guest.

My wife, ever pragmatic, couldn't help but laugh when I vented my frustrations.

"You have zero sense of how the world works," she said, her words sharp but not entirely untrue. "You thought people would help you just because your grandfather helped them decades ago? Wake up. This is not the same world, and they're not the same people anymore. And it was your grandfather who had helped them not you."

Her laughter stung, but the truth behind her words stung even more. She wasn't trying to belittle me — she was trying to shake me out of my naivety. She had always been my biggest critic and, at the same time, my staunchest ally. And even though her words felt harsh, I knew they came from a place of love and practicality.

For days, her words echoed in my mind. "Zero sense of how the world works." Was that who I had become? A dreamer disconnected from reality? Or was there still a way to bridge the gap between my vision and the harsh truths of the world?

CHAPTER TEN

Failing miserably at raising support from the people I thought would help, I turned to my friends.

These were the people who had seen me at my best and worst, who had shared in my laughter and my struggles. They knew me beyond the surface, beyond the stories I carried and the dreams I clung to. Surely, they would understand my vision and lend a hand, even if it was just in small ways.

A couple of them did. Their support, no matter how modest, felt like a lifeline in a storm. Their actions weren't just gestures of support; they were affirmations of belief—in me, in the dream, in the possibility of what this Trust could achieve. I will forever remain grateful to them, and I'll carry their kindness as a debt of honor. If ever they need me, in this lifetime or in countless lifetimes to come, I will be at their service without a second thought.

But then there were the others.

Many of my friends made promises — big, bold promises that once again filled me with excitement and hope.

"Don't worry," they would say. "I'll help you raise the funds. Just give me some time."

Their words were laced with conviction, and for a brief moment, I allowed myself to believe that help was truly on the way.

One friend in particular made a grand promise to contribute a significant amount.

"Consider it done, Bro," he said, his tone brimming with confidence.

For days, I clung to those words like a lifeline. I planned my next steps, thinking about how that contribution would help me take the trust forward. But when the time came, nothing happened. I reached out, hesitant but hopeful, only to be met with a casual, almost dismissive response: "Oh, I forgot about that. Let me get back to you."

He never did.

Once again, it wasn't the lack of contributions that hurt the most — it was the gap between their words and their actions. I understand that they have commitments, family responsibilities, and lives of their own to look after. They aren't obligated to share my vision or shoulder my burden. I truly do understand that.

But they were my friends. They could have said no straight to my face, or at least a simple – "I can't right now or ever", and I would have understood. A straightforward rejection, though painful, would have been honest. It would have allowed me to move forward without false hope, without planning around promises that were never going to materialize. Instead, I was left dangling, caught between their words and their silence, never knowing where I truly stood with them.

My Wife was watching everything quietly from the sidelines, saying little but observing everything. I didn't need her to voice what she was thinking — I could feel it in the air, in her eyes. Deep down, I know how big of a disappointment I must have been to her. Though she wasn't saying anything outright, her silence spoke volumes.

This was the woman who had stood by me through all my struggles, who had seen me fail and pick myself back up countless times. And now, here I was again, grappling with rejection after rejection, clinging to scraps of support that seemed to slip through my fingers.

Her quiet presence was a constant reminder of the stakes — not just for me, but for us, for our family. I imagined her thoughts, her unspoken worries. Was this just another of my fleeting ideas, destined to fade away like the others? Was I putting us at risk with this dream of mine, dragging us down a path that seemed to lead nowhere?

And then there was my job, which by now I despised from every corner of my heart.

It had become a symbol of everything I wanted to leave behind — the suffocating routines, the hollow ambitions, the lack of purpose. Each morning, dragging myself out of bed and heading to the office felt like walking into a cage, locking myself away for hours only to emerge more drained than before.

I had stayed in the job because it was practical, because it paid the bills, and because it was what was expected of me. But the weight of its monotony and emptiness had grown unbearable. The very thought of stepping into that building each day felt like walking into a battlefield where I was losing ground with every passing moment. Sitting through meetings that revolved around how to lure in more students—strategies designed not to educate or empower but to fill seats and maximize profits — was unbearable.

Every social media design that landed on my desk for approval, depicting a smiling student with a hefty job package, was like a slap in the face. I knew those glossy promises weren't true. They were carefully constructed illusions meant to sell dreams, not deliver them. They were designed to lure in unsuspecting parents and hopeful students, offering them a vision of success that this institution had neither the intention nor the capacity to fulfill.

And then there were the budgets. Every budget I had to prepare felt like an act of betrayal. In one column, I had to fill in the collection from students for an event —money taken in the name of providing them with opportunities, exposure, and experiences. In the next column, I had to calculate the bare minimum we should spend on that same event, ensuring the numbers balanced in a way that maximized the institution's profit. The students' contributions weren't investments in their future — they were revenue streams for the institution.

Every time I typed those figures; it was like a knife to my heart. I could picture the parents, trusting us with their hard-earned money, believing that these events would bring their children closer to their dreams. I could picture the students, full of hope and ambition, unaware that their education was being reduced to a balance sheet.

And above all, it was the pretense that wore me down—the constant act of pretending to care about things I no longer believed in. Smiling politely as decisions were made that prioritized revenue over integrity. Every day, I felt a little piece of myself eroding, as though my soul was being chipped away, one fake bill and one false promise at a time.

I hated what I had become — a man trapped between societal obligations and the desire to break free and build something meaningful.

I carried that weight everywhere I went. It wasn't just the disappointment of others I was wrestling with — it was my own. I couldn't ignore the quiet voice in my head that questioned whether I had what it took to see this dream through. It whispered doubts, reminding me of all the times I had failed before.

There were moments when the frustration became almost unbearable. I would sit alone at night, my head in my hands, questioning whether it was time to give up. To neatly fold the dream away, label it unrealistic, and push it to the back of my mind, where so many other unfulfilled ambitions had already been buried.

There were moments when the frustration became almost unbearable. I would sit alone at night, my head in my hands, questioning whether it was time to give up. To neatly fold the dream away, label it unrealistic, and push it to the back of my mind, where so many other unfulfilled ambitions had already been buried.

But something deep within me refused to let that happen. That's the thing about Purpose—it doesn't fade in the face of obstacles. It is not just an idea but a divine whisper, a calling that refuses to be silenced. No matter how improbable it seems, once you truly recognize it, even after a million failures, you cannot accept that it cannot be done.

And I believe from the deepest core of my heart that the Mother Divine had shown me this path—had pulled me out of the depths of despair and illuminated this vision for me. I had felt her presence in the quiet moments, guiding me, urging me forward, even when the world seemed to push back at every turn.

I couldn't shake the feeling that she held the trump card in her hand, waiting for the right moment to play it. It was as though she was testing me, challenging me to prove my commitment and perseverance. Every setback, every rejection, every moment of doubt felt like part of a greater design—a way of preparing me for what was to come.

The thought gave me strength. It reminded me that giving up wasn't an option—not because of pride or ego, but because I knew deep down that this path was meant for me.

In those moments of doubt, I clung to the belief that the Divine doesn't place a dream in your heart without also giving you the strength to pursue it. I didn't know how or when, but I trusted that the pieces would fall into place — if only I could keep going.

CHAPTER ELEVEN

Days slipped by in an uneasy blur, each one bringing fresh struggles, yet offering no respite. Whatever money I had raised from my friends was exhausted in the hope of raising more capital. I was down to the last 25K in my Trust's account.

One evening, my wife sat beside me as the harsh white glow of the tube light flickered uncertainly over the papers strewn across my bed. Her voice was gentle, yet there was a firmness in her tone, a kind of quiet resolve that only someone who had watched from the sidelines for too long could have.

"You've given it your all," she said. "Maybe it's time to wrap this up and withdraw the money. You can always start again later, in a better situation."

Her words stung more than I cared to admit. It wasn't just about money — her plea carried the weight of something deeper. She wasn't merely asking me to pull the plug on this venture; she was asking me to acknowledge defeat.

But how could I? A few of my friends had contributed toward this cause, believing in the vision as much as I did. Wrapping it up would mean deceiving them, betraying the trust they had placed in me. It would mean admitting that all the late nights, the endless strategizing, the countless sacrifices had led to nothing.

"Listen to me," she pressed. "If you want, return their money. We can start later."

I looked at her, my chest tight with a familiar defiance. "I started this Trust in the name of Mother Divine," I said. "By her inspiration. And only if she commands, I will wrap it up."

My wife let out a short laugh, shaking her head at my unwavering resolve. Or stupidity.

"Having faith is one thing," she said. "Blind faith is another altogether. Mother Divine did not come to you asking to start this. It was your decision. You named it after her, and that I respect. But it has now started to take a toll on us."

She was right. And I knew it.

My job consumed my days, forcing me to leave home at eight in the morning and return by six in the evening. That left precious little time for my initiative. Over the past months, my iPad had become my world—my constant companion, my refuge, my battleground. Every free moment was spent devising ways to raise funds. I scoured government websites for grants, poured over countless business strategies, and subscribed to digital tools—ChatGPT, Canva, WhatsApp API, social media ads—all in a desperate attempt to crack the code of sustainability. But nothing yielded the breakthrough I needed.

Meanwhile, my presence at home had become more of a formality than a reality. Conversations were brief, my responses distracted and half-hearted. My wife had been watching me slip away, inch by inch, into an obsession that was now draining the both of us.

And yet, despite everything—despite the exhaustion, the repeated failures, the creeping doubt—there was one thing I couldn't bring myself to do.

I wasn't ready to give up.

Each day, I had begun waking at five in the morning, despite our bedtime being past eleven. Winters in the hills are unforgiving, yet I took my bath before sunrise, completed my prayers, and by the time my family awoke, I would already be seated on the sofa, iPad in hand, searching for ways to keep my vision alive. I wrote letters to foundations, explaining the impact this initiative could have, detailing the dreams it could bring to life.

None of them replied.

Desperation had driven me to a place I never thought I'd reach — The weight of failure pressed against my ribs as I considered asking my father to mortgage our ancestral land, a lifeline carved from the history of my family. For a fleeting moment, the idea of demanding my share outright crossed my mind, the thought lingering like a shadow, tempting yet repulsive.

Even now, I can't pinpoint what held me back. Perhaps it was the whisper of something greater than myself—Mother Divine, intervening in silence, urging me to pause before making an irreversible choice.

New Year's Eve arrived like an empty promise, flickering with distant fireworks and hollow cheer. It passed, indifferent to my turmoil, leaving behind the same relentless struggles, the same unbearable weight of stagnation.

Every morning, I woke with dread, suffocated by the routine that had become my prison. In the depths of that wretchedness, bitterness seeped into my thoughts, and I even cursed my grandfather. He had once stood at a crossroads where he could have changed everything, could have rewritten our fate — but he hadn't. And now, I bore the weight of choices never made.

Everything led to a quite slow collapse. By the middle of January, I fell tremendously ill. Some opportunistic Viruses, harsh winter, and the routine of taking a bath way before sunrise were to blame. It was so bad that even my spiritual practice, a routine I had been maintaining for past eight months broke leaving me heartbroken beyond repair.

But Divine has a way of intervening when least expected, her touch subtle yet undeniable. As I lay in bed, buried beneath two quilts, fever gripping my body and exhaustion weighing me down, the thought of surrendering fully crept into my mind. I had begun to accept defeat, to let the burden slip away. But then, without warning, something shattered the stillness of the night. A force — intangible, yet undeniable — jerked me awake. It was abrupt, almost violent, as if unseen hands had reached into my very core and shaken me. My heart pounded in my chest, the fever's haze momentarily lifting, and in that instant, my mind, found an unexpected clarity. And a single thought crystallized in my mind: It's my dream. Just as Pandit Madan Mohan Malviya had. Just as Rabindranath Tagore had. And just as Sir Sayyed had.

If they had dared to dream against all odds, then so could I. They had built legacies out of sheer determination, had sculpted institutions from nothing but vision and grit. Was my faith any less? Was my purpose any smaller?

A renewed energy coursed through me, fragile yet unwavering. The fever, the exhaustion, the crippling doubt—none of it mattered anymore. What mattered was the path ahead, the belief that had refused to let go of me even when I had nearly let go of it. I would rise. I would fight. I would find a way to make it happen. Just as they had.

It was time to stop waiting. It was time to take the first step. Again.

That morning after tea, I started contemplating again.

I needed to travel. City to city, face to face, I needed to meet people, just as Malaviya had. So, what if couple of businessmen refused to believe in me. The world has not ended with them.

I would make them see the dream.

Feel the urgency.

Believe in the cause as much as I did.

It was time to take the battle to the world.

That was the question I needed an answer to. And it came instantly.

I had always been an avid reader since childhood. Books had been my greatest companions, shaping my thoughts and fueling my imagination. I knew firsthand the power a book could hold—the way it could inspire, inform, and even ignite a movement.

And I had some experience writing, too. Back in 2017, I had participated in Amazon's Pen to Publish contest, pouring my heart into a full-length novel. It had been a challenge, but I had completed it, proving to myself that I could commit to a story, see it through, and put my thoughts into words that resonated.

This time, it wouldn't be a novel. It would be my story.

I had found my answer. I would write. I would tell my story. And through it, I would make the people believe.

It was time to stop waiting. It was time to take the first step.

Though, I had written before, but this was different. This was not just an entry in a contest or a casual attempt at storytelling—this was my truth, raw and unfiltered.

My fingers hovered over the keyboard, and for a moment, doubt crept in. Could I really do this? Could I bare my soul in a way that would move people, in a way that would make them see what I saw?

I shook off the hesitation and began.

I started by tracing the steps that had brought me here. The long nights, the relentless pursuit of a vision that had seemed impossible at times. And created a time line. A one pager that I would turn into words.

But the question lingered—would people listen? Would they believe? Would they see the dream as I did?

I had no way of knowing. But that was not my concern anymore. My task was to write, to speak, to share. The rest, I would leave to fate, to destiny, to the unseen force that had carried me this far.

The journey was no longer just mine. It belonged to whoever was willing to walk it with me. And so I started writing.

And once again, Mother Divine surprised me with her plans. At my job, an unexpected situation arose — Despite my best performance, the management suddenly decided that I should step down from my post as Director Admissions and Finance Officer and return to the teaching cadre. I had always loved teaching for the nobility it carried, the ability to shape young minds and inspire, but stepping down from a statutory post without any justification and taking up an inferior position did not sit well with my conscience.

So, I decided to be honest about my aspirations.

I explained to them my plans of doing something on my own, of pursuing a vision that had been growing inside me for years. And with that, I tendered my resignation, on 27th Jan 2025 marking the final step toward my freedom.

CHAPTER TWELVE

Today is the 29th of January. And here I am, staring at the last chapter of my journey, knowing full well that it's not an ending at all. It's the beginning. A spark. I've spent pages talking about the past, digging through memories, peeling back the layers of struggle and transformation. But this? This is different. This is where the story takes a turn—not just mine, but maybe yours too.

See, I have this dream. A wild, stubborn, relentless dream that refuses to sit quietly in the back of my mind. A school. But not the kind with dull lectures, rigid rules, and a focus on churning out perfect report cards. No, I want to build something different. A place where kids don't just learn—they grow, they discover, they become. A space filled with curiosity, adventure, and the kind of learning that actually matters.

Picture this: a sprawling campus,like the one you see in movies, spacious classrooms, laughter echoing across an open playground, a swimming pool where kids learn confidence, self-defense training that builds strength — not just physical, but mental. This isn't about ticking boxes. It's about preparing young minds for life. Because let's be honest, the world doesn't care how well you memorized a textbook. It cares about how you think, how you solve problems, how you navigate chaos without losing yourself.

I want a curriculum that goes beyond equations and grammar rules. Yes, those are important, but so is critical thinking. So is understanding emotions, standing up for what's right. That's the kind of foundation I want. A school where Music, arts, physical education are not afterthought, but as essentials. I want a school whose alumnus will not have any need for coaching or tuitions. Every child will walk out of school knowing who he is, what he loves, and how to shape his future on his own.

But I can't do this alone.

No real change ever happens in isolation. It takes a tribe, a collective, a group of people who see the same vision and say, "Let's make this happen." To bring this school to life, I will need more than just passion; I'll need resources, planning, and a shared commitment to building something truly extraordinary.

As I am from Himachal Pradesh, I envision this school being rooted in the heart of this beautiful state. It will be a residential school that will draw children from every corner of the country, providing them with a safe and enriching environment where they can grow, learn, and thrive. I wish to name this institution People's Public School.

To make this a reality, I will need at least 15 acres of land. In addition to the land, a fully-fledged residential school will require significant infrastructure. This will include classrooms, dormitories, sports facilities, arts and music studios, dining areas, staff accommodations, and much more. The infrastructure costs for such a project will be substantial, covering everything from construction to utilities, educational resources, and campus amenities.

But one has to take baby steps before he could leap.

I know that raising funds for such a grand endeavor will be a challenging and painful process. That's why I've decided that whatever I can generate by selling this book will go directly into the construction of the elementary wing of the school. Every purchase, every contribution, will be a brick in the foundation of this dream.

In the later stages, if it is in accordance with divine will, I will take this vision even further — transforming it into a fully-fledged university that will stand shoulder to shoulder with the top institutions of India and the world. A place where the pursuit of knowledge and self-discovery are not just academic goals but the foundation of a lifelong journey. This institution will not merely compete; it will lead, inspire, and redefine what it means to be truly educated in the 21st century.

This dream now belongs to everyone who dares to believe in a future that's better, brighter, and more meaningful. A world where education doesn't just fill minds with facts, but shapes the very future itself. So now, I ask you: Are you in? Because this is not the end — it's only the beginning. A beginning to something far greater than we could imagine alone. Let's walk this path together, step by step, building a foundation that will last for generations.

You've already made an impact simply by purchasing this book, contributing more than enough to this cause. But there's still more to be done. If any part of this resonates with you, if you believe that education should be a force that nurtures mind and ignites passions, I invite you to be a part of this movement. Whether it's a financial contribution, sharing your expertise, or simply telling someone who needs to hear this message, every bit helps.

Together, we can build something that transcends the ordinary, creating a legacy that will leave a lasting mark on the world.

In the pages that follow, you'll find a QR Code that will lead you to a page where you can contribute in your own way. Your support — no matter how big or small — is the spark that can ignite a transformation. To maintain transparency in financial operations I have made the Finance Tracker of the Trust public. You can access it at www.sbgu.org in Financial Tabs in the main menu.

And now, let me close this with the title that perfectly captures the essence of this manifesto:

I Have a Dream.

And It Can Be Yours Too.

Powered by

Razorpay

G Pay

paytm

SRI BALA GURUKULAM
FOUNDATION TRUST

Your Support Matters

www.ingramcontent.com/pod-product-compliance
Lightning Source LLC
LaVergne TN
LVHW091223150826
845673LV00003B/986

* 9 7 9 8 8 9 7 2 4 0 7 7 7 *